HISPANIC AMERICA

1898 TO
WORLD WAR II

BY

ROGER E. HERNÁNDEZ

Marshall Cavendish
Benchmark
New York

Thanks to José Guevara-Escudero, Ph.D., CFP, professor of Latin American Studies in the History department at Pace University, for his expert reading of this manuscript.

MARSHALL CAVENDISH BENCHMARK
99 WHITE PLAINS ROAD
TARRYTOWN, NEW YORK 10591-5502
www.marshallcavendish.us

Text copyright © 2010 by Marshall Cavendish Corporation

LIBRARY OF CONGRESS CATALOGING-IN-PUBLICATION DATA
Hernández, Roger E.
1898 to World War II / by Roger E. Hernández.
p. cm. — (Hispanic America)
Includes bibliographical references and index.
Summary: "Provides comprehensive information on the history of the Spanish coming to the United States, focusing on the time from 1898 to the start of World War II"—Provided by publisher.
ISBN 978-0-7614-4176-2
1. Hispanic Americans—History—20th century—Juvenile literature. 2. Puerto Ricans—New York (State)—New York—History—20th century—Juvenile literature. 3. Hispanic Americans—Florida—Tampa—History—20th century—Juvenile literature. 4. Mexican Americans—History—20th century—Juvenile literature. 5. New Mexico—Civilization—Hispanic influences—Juvenile literature. 6. United States—Ethnic relations—History—20th century—Juvenile literature.
I. Title.
E184.S75H474 2009
973'.0468—dc22
2008041140

Photo research by Tracey Engel

Cover: Lewis Wickes Hine/CORBIS
Title page: Palace of the Governors (MNM/DCA): #050609 Back cover: CORBIS
The photographs in this book are used by permission and through the courtesy of:
Alamy: Pictorial Press Ltd, 14; AA World Travel Library, 24. *AP/Wide World Photos*: 7. *The Center for American History, The University of Texas at Austin*: The Robert Runyon Photograph Collection, 00096, 50. *Corbis*: 6, 44, 70-71; MAPS.com, 9; Bettmann, 16, 17, 18-19, 22, 27, 55, 57, 66; Hulton-Deutsch Collection, 40; Dorothea Lange, 47; C. L., Forsling, 66. *The Granger Collection, New York*: 28, 46. *Library of Congress*: Prints & Photographs Division, LC-DIG-npcc 19554, 52; LC-DIG-fsa-8b26837, 58. *Daniel Modell*: 12. *The New York Public Library*: Picture Collection, The Branch Libraries, Astor, Lenox and Tilden Foundations, 4. *North Wind Picture Archives*: 11, 42. *Palace of the Governors (MNM/DCA)* : #022468, 60; #139519, 63; #050609, 69. *State Library and Archives of Florida*: 30-31; 33, 36-37; 39.

EDITOR: Joy Bean   PUBLISHER: Michelle Bisson
ART DIRECTOR: Anahid Hamparian   SERIES DESIGNER: Kristen Branch

Printed in Malaysia
1 3 5 6 4 2

CONTENTS

CHAPTER ONE

PUERTO RICAN PIONEERS IN NEW YORK

THE PERIOD BETWEEN THE END OF THE Spanish-American War and the start of World War II lasted from 1898 to 1939. This period may seem like a forgotten era in the history of Hispanics in the United States. In the Spanish-American War, the United States defeated Spain and took what remained of the Spanish colonial empire, including Cuba and Puerto Rico. After this dramatic time, the country paid little attention to Hispanic American communities. Instead, major crises grabbed the attention of Americans. They were concerned about World War I, the *Great Depression*, and the rise of *fascism* in foreign countries. Americans were concerned about immigration, but the newcomers that worried some people back then were not Hispanic.

Opposite: During the Spanish-American War, the United States fought Spain for control of the Spanish empire.

5

Still, important developments in those years helped shape the Hispanic Americans of today. In California and Texas, more than a million Mexicans arrived. They were fleeing the violence and economic chaos of the Mexican Revolution, which began in 1910. This was the first mass migration of Mexicans to the United States. Nearby New Mexico, with its centuries-old Hispanic population, became a state in 1912. This was six decades after the United States conquered the territory in the U.S.-Mexican War of 1846.

Rival communities of Cubans and Spaniards had settled in Tampa, Florida, in the 1880s. During Cuba's struggle for independence from Spain, these communities changed their priorities after the United States helped the Cubans in the Spanish-American War. With the defeat of Spain and

A Mexican family stands in the front yard of their thatch-roofed house in Texas, near the border of Mexico.

the independence of Cuba in 1902, the political organizations disappeared from Tampa and the focus shifted to the booming cigar-making industry. The neighborhood of Ybor City became a vibrant immigrant community until the Great Depression.

In New York, the first pioneering immigrants arrived from Puerto Rico, an island that did not become independent after the United States took it from Spain. Puerto Rico remained under American control, with increasing home rule as the years went on.

WAR ENDS IN PUERTO RICO

On the night of February 15, 1898, there was an explosion aboard the U.S. battleship *Maine*, anchored in Havana

Lifeboats rescue surviving crewmen of the wrecked USS *Maine* after an explosion destroyed the battleship.

Harbor, Cuba. This event set off the Spanish-American War. The attack killed 266 American sailors. An angry U.S. government blamed Spain for the explosion and declared war that April.

Spain had ruled Cuba and Puerto Rico since Columbus claimed both islands in 1492. As years went by, native-born Cubans and Puerto Ricans sought to rule themselves instead of being ruled by the colonial government of Spain. Many Americans sympathized with their cause. They recalled overthrowing British colonial rule during the Revolutionary War. However, many Americans believed that the United States should influence the affairs of islands close to Florida, such as Cuba and Puerto Rico.

Cuba was larger and richer than Puerto Rico. Rebels in Cuba had fought Spain in two major wars, while there had been little fighting in Puerto Rico. So it was the struggle in Cuba that received the most attention in the United States. And when the United States went to war against Spain, Cuba was the big prize at the center of the fighting, not Puerto Rico. This is because during the four hundred years of Spanish rule in the Caribbean, Cuba had been the commercial, political, and military center of the empire, while Puerto Rico was less important.

Still, Americans wanted to push Spain out of Puerto Rico as well. The first three thousand American soldiers landed in Puerto Rico on July 25, 1898. By that time, Spanish troops had already surrendered Cuba's eastern

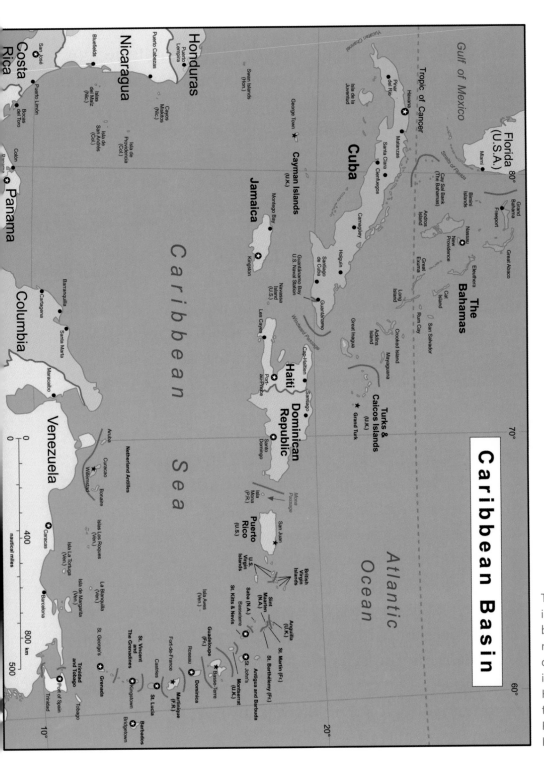

Caribbean Basin

The Caribbean includes a number of island nations off the coast of Florida, including Cuba, Haiti, Jamaica, the Dominican Republic, and Puerto Rico.

province to U.S. forces, and the war was practically over. In Puerto Rico, Americans and Spaniards fought small battles near the cities of Coamo and Mayagüez, but the people of Puerto Rico greeted American soldiers as liberators. Then, on August 12, Spain and the United States signed an *armistice*. This agreement ended the fighting and gave the United States possession of Cuba and Puerto Rico.

U.S. RULE BEGINS

At first, Puerto Rico was governed by direct U.S. military rule. Four army generals governed the island between 1898 and 1900. That year, the Foraker Act was approved in Washington, D.C. This was the first of several U.S. laws that put Puerto Rico on a political path toward its current status as a *commonwealth*.

The Foraker Act stated that Puerto Rico would be provided with a civilian governor appointed by the U.S. president. The island would have a house of representatives with thirty-five members elected by Puerto Rican males, as well as members of the U.S. Congress. Puerto Ricans would not become American citizens.

Some Puerto Ricans objected. They felt their island was still governed like a colony. They would not make their own political decisions. Instead, U.S. officials in Washington, D.C., would rule the island. Among these objectors was Luis Muñoz Rivera, one of the best-known politicians in the history of Puerto Rico. Before the war, in 1887, he became the

Once the United States won the Spanish-American War, Puerto Rico became a commonwealth of the U.S. Here, U.S. troops enter Puerto Rico.

PUERTO RICAN PIONEERS IN NEW YORK

leader of the Autonomist Party, which sought to keep Puerto Rico part of Spain but with more local powers. Ten years later, the Spanish government finally decided to let Puerto Ricans have more power. Muñoz Rivera was part of the new government. However, just a few days after he was sworn in as chief of the cabinet, the United States defeated Spain and installed the first of the military governors.

Luis Muñoz Rivera fought for more rights for Puerto Ricans after the United States took control of the island.

Muñoz Rivera continued to push for more self-rule. In 1901, he moved to New York to continue his campaign. He established the bilingual newspaper *The Puerto Rican Herald*, in which he criticized the Foraker Act as undemocratic. After moving back to Puerto Rico in 1904, he was elected to the local legislature in 1906. In 1910, he was elected as resident commissioner to the U.S. House of Representatives.

In Congress, Muñoz Rivera continued his fight for more self-rule. His work there finally led to the Jones Act of 1917. This act established a stronger, *two-chamber legislature*. It also granted U.S. citizenship to Puerto

Ricans in an arrangement that persists to this day, allowing Puerto Ricans who live in one of the fifty states to vote for president of the United States, but not those who live in Puerto Rico.

Muñoz Rivera did not get everything he wanted, but he did achieve increased local rule for Puerto Rico. His son, Luis Muñoz Marín, would build on that legacy and gain still more local power for Puerto Rico in the 1930s and 1940s. Meanwhile, the people of the island took the first steps in what would later be a large migration to New York City.

EARLY NEWYORICANS

There are some 3.7 million people of Puerto Rican ancestry living in the fifty states and another 3.9 million in Puerto Rico itself. In other words, almost half of all Puerto Ricans live outside Puerto Rico.

That is because the island has long been poor, and its people emigrate to look for better opportunities. In *The Puerto Rican Migrant in New York City*, author Lawrence R. Chenault wrote that in the 1930s, the average wage for workers in six different industries in Puerto Rico was a little more than six dollars a week. Meanwhile, the same jobs in the continental United States paid an average of thirty dollars a week—five times more. Even worse, "The laborer in Puerto Rico buys food at the same price or possibly a slightly higher price. . . . The worker must spend practically his entire income for food, and even then lives in a half-starved condition."

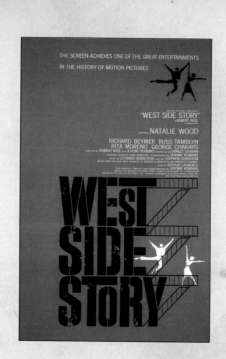

PUERTO RICAN CULTURE

It took a while for U.S. popular culture to recognize Puerto Rico. In the early 1900s, there had been a craze for the tango, an Argentinean dance. In the 1930s, band leaders Don Azpiazu and Xavier Cugat popularized Cuban music—but Puerto Rican music did not go mainstream.

In his 2007 book *Boricua Power*, author José Ramón Sánchez wrote that in the period between 1936 and 1955 Hollywood producers made just 15 movies that had any mention of Puerto Rico. This was compared to 605 films in which Mexico was a presence, 157 that featured Argentina, and 84 in which Cuba appeared.

It was not until *West Side Story*—the 1957 Broadway musical that became an Oscar-winning movie in 1961—that Puerto Rico made it big in American popular culture.

Those were the workers lucky enough to have jobs in a city. In 1930, the 52 percent of Puerto Ricans who worked on farms were even poorer. Most of them did not own the land they worked. Instead, they were laborers employed by big landowners. These landless peasants, called *jíbaros*, lived in desperately poor conditions. Chenault wrote, "Not always is [the farmworker] able to provide rice, beans, codfish, and vegetables in sufficient quantities. Occasionally, depending upon the work available, he may have pork, milk or flour. After a cup or two of black coffee for breakfast, he may walk several miles to his work, and work until dusk for less than a dollar."

In such conditions, even working-class wages in the United States must have seemed like wild riches. "Relatives and friends already in the United States exert a strong influence," Chenault wrote. "Almost everyone has some friend or relative . . . who has gone to the United States and secured employment."

As U.S. citizens, Puerto Ricans could come and go as they pleased. All they needed was the money for travel. Laws passed in the 1920s drastically cut the number of immigrants allowed to enter the country. This did not affect Puerto Ricans. They could travel from their island to New York just as legally as an American citizen from New Jersey.

Author José Ramón Sánchez wrote about one of the largest and earliest waves of Puerto Ricans in the United States. This wave included 75,000 men whom the U.S. government contracted to work "on behalf of the war effort"

A slum in San Juan, Puerto Rico, shows the living conditions from which some of the families were trying to escape when they left their homes to live in the United States.

during World War I. They were paid only thirty-five cents an hour and many were "ill treated."

Government contracting was a fairly common practice over the first two decades of the twentieth century. Puerto Ricans labored on Hawaiian farms, New Orleans docks, and elsewhere. These contract workers were returned to Puerto Rico after their jobs ended. They were not immigrants who settled in a new land.

There were some—but not many—true Puerto Rican immigrants in the first few decades after the United States took control of the island. In 1910, the U.S. Census Bureau counted only 1,513 people born in Puerto Rico living in the continental United States. By 1920, there were 11,811. And by 1930, the figure was 52,774. The growth was steady, and the figure would have been larger had it included the children of Puerto Rican parents born on the mainland. Yet there were few Puerto Ricans compared to the millions of European immigrants who arrived during the same decades. Puerto Rico was so poor that few people could afford the journey by boat.

Many of the Puerto Ricans who came to the United States to work were paid only thirty-five cents an hour for the hard labor they did.

The majority of Puerto Ricans who did take the journey went to New York. In 1930, for instance, 87 percent of all Puerto Ricans in the United States lived in New York. Why did they not go to Florida, which is closer to Puerto Rico and has similar weather? Or Texas and California, which are farther away but also have relatively warm weather? Chenault has suggested several reasons. Puerto Ricans saw the southern states, where African Americans already occupied the lowest-paying jobs, as "a place of little opportunity." In heavily Hispanic Tampa, Cubans already filled the higher-paying jobs in the cigar-making industry. New York, in contrast, had many available factory jobs.

Eventually, Puerto Ricans from New York began calling themselves Newyorricans.

SETTLING IN NUEVA YORK

Making a living in Nueva York—Spanish for "New York"—turned out not to be as easy as some of the Puerto Ricans newcomers had hoped. The cold winters were a shock to people accustomed to a warm tropical climate. They had never needed heavy coats or heaters for their homes. Another adjustment was the enormous city of New York itself.

Up until the late 1920s, many Puerto Ricans found employment in the cigar-making factories of New York. Sánchez says that in 1920, about 60 percent of the 7,364 Puerto Ricans in New York worked in the cigar industry. They were among the highest-paid industrial laborers in the city. But the glory days of tobacco employment did not last. In the mid-1920s, factories started to use machines to make cigars, and tens of thousands of workers found themselves out of a job.

Outside of the cigar industry, Puerto Ricans found themselves at a disadvantage during the Great Depression of the 1930s. Few jobs were available to anybody, natives and immigrants alike. Another problem was language and education.

Jobs were scarce during the Great Depression. People without jobs often waited in long lines for bread to feed their families.

PUERTO RICAN PIONEERS IN NEW YORK

According to the 1930 census, about 80 percent of the people in Puerto Rico did not speak English. Forty percent were illiterate, in both English and Spanish. Most English speakers in Puerto Rico belonged to the educated upper classes, which were less likely to move to New York. This meant the immigrant population probably had an even higher percentage of non-English speakers—and of people who could not speak or write any language.

Racial *discrimination* was also a problem. Although some Puerto Ricans were white descendants of Spanish colonists, many others came from enslaved Africans brought to Puerto Rico generations earlier. Yet others had mixed white and black ancestry. Like all immigrants, Puerto Ricans encountered discrimination from Americans who disliked all "foreigners," no matter what race.

Some Puerto Ricans went back to the island, disappointed. From 1931 to 1933, in the depths of the Great Depression, about three thousand more people returned to Puerto Rico than people who moved from the island to the continental United States. In addition to escaping the poor economic conditions, many Puerto Ricans complained that the weather was too cold.

POLITICAL CHANGES

Still, the majority of Puerto Ricans stayed and worked hard. Even if the immigrants themselves never learned English, their children did. Slowly, they began to acquire political power. Until the 1940s, the Puerto Rican community in New York was not large enough for politicians to consider it a major voting block. However, the activism of the cigar workers, and then the establishment of Puerto Rican political and social organizations, attracted the attention of powerful figures such as Mayor Fiorello La Guardia. Author José Ramón Sánchez wrote that at least forty-four such groups were founded between 1918 and 1940 including four Spanish-language newspapers. One of them survives today as *El Diario/La Prensa* (*The Daily Press*), founded in 1918.

By 1940, there were 61,000 Puerto Ricans in New York. Half of them were registered to vote. Three years earlier, Puerto Rican voters had helped elect Oscar García Rivera to the New York State *assembly*. Rivera was the first Puerto Rican elected to public office in the United States.

There were changes on the island, too. Luis Muñoz Marín, son of Muñoz Rivera, carried on his father's work of gaining more rights for Puerto Rico. In 1938, he helped found the Partido Popular Democrático, or Popular Democratic Party, which remains one of the island's three leading political parties today. Muñoz Marín led the fight to change the system by which the U.S. president appointed the governor of Puerto Rico. In 1948, he became the island's first democratically elected governor.

Six years later, Muñoz Marín was the main force in adopting a new Puerto Rican constitution and redefining the island's relationship with the United States. Under his

Luis Muñoz Marín is the son of Luis Muñoz Rivera. Marín also fought for more rights for Puerto Ricans. Here, he is addressing the press while governor of Puerto Rico.

guidance, Puerto Rico officially became a commonwealth of the United States (in Spanish, *estado libre asociado*, or free associated state). The arrangement said that Puerto Rico was not one of the fifty states, but neither was it an independent country. It was a mix of both. For instance, Puerto Rico fields its own Olympic teams under its flag, a source of great pride. But it does not have its own foreign policy—the United States governs its relations with other countries.

The commonwealth arrangement remains controversial.

Some critics say it is unfair that Puerto Ricans in Puerto Rico cannot vote for the U.S. president. These critics formed a political party that seeks statehood for the island. Others say Puerto Rico should be a *sovereign* nation. These people formed a party that favors independence from the United States. In four *referenda*—held in 1967, 1991, 1993 and 1998—Puerto Rican voters upheld the commonwealth status. Statehood was a close second, and independence came in far behind. Puerto Ricans in the continental United States as well as on the island continue to debate the future of their land.

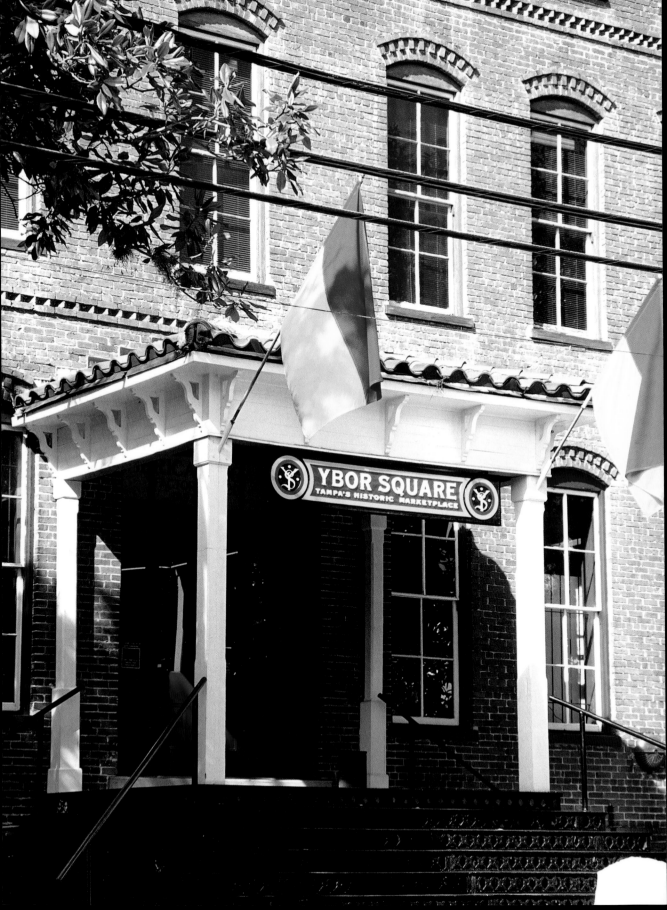

CHAPTER TWO

THRIVING TAMPA

BETWEEN 1900 AND 1929, TAMPA'S SPANISH-speaking neighborhood, called Ybor City, was in many ways a model immigrant community. Unlike many other immigrant neighborhoods of those years, it was not a slum of *tenement housing* and widespread poverty. Instead, it was a solid working-class neighborhood where many people found well-paying jobs in the cigar factories. Spanish-speaking Tampa became prosperous enough to open several social clubs. The clubs had impressive buildings where members held cultural events and feasts with traditional foods.

Ybor City was founded by Vicente Martínez Ybor, a Spaniard who was raised in Cuba when it was a colony of Spain. He started a cigar factory in Havana, Cuba's capital, but the Ten Years' War for Cuban independence forced him

Opposite:
Ybor City in Tampa, Florida, was a popular destination for many Spanish-speaking immigrants.

to relocate to Key West, Florida, in 1868. Over the next few years, Ybor faced *striking* workers, a lack of a steady freshwater supply, and transportation problems. In 1885, he decided to build a new factory near Tampa, which had a population of about seven hundred. He wanted to build not just a factory, but also thousands of homes for the families of workers. Ybor wanted a company town, where workers had fewer complaints about their bosses.

In 1887, Ybor City officially became part of Tampa. At this time, the population was about three thousand. Tampa kept growing. There were nearly 38,000 inhabitants by 1910 and more than 100,000 in 1930.

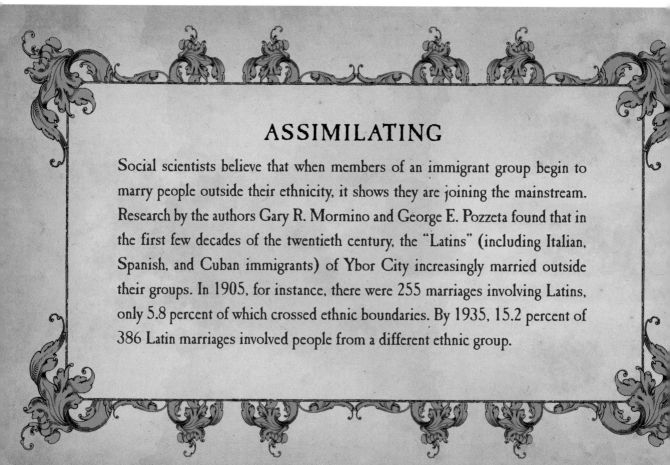

ASSIMILATING

Social scientists believe that when members of an immigrant group begin to marry people outside their ethnicity, it shows they are joining the mainstream. Research by the authors Gary R. Mormino and George E. Pozzeta found that in the first few decades of the twentieth century, the "Latins" (including Italian, Spanish, and Cuban immigrants) of Ybor City increasingly married outside their groups. In 1905, for instance, there were 255 marriages involving Latins, only 5.8 percent of which crossed ethnic boundaries. By 1935, 15.2 percent of 386 Latin marriages involved people from a different ethnic group.

SPAIN AND CUBA: FAMILY RIVALS

Ybor City was home to two Spanish-speaking communities—people from Cuba and people from Spain. According to the 1910 census, about 3,800 residents of Tampa were born in Cuba and about 2,400 in Spain. In 1930, the Cuban-born population reached more than 5,000 and the Spanish population was 3,500.

Sometimes Cubans and Spaniards got along. Other times—especially during Cuba's struggle for independence in the nineteenth century—the two communities saw each other as rivals. Through the 1880s and 1890s, Tampa (along with Key West) had been a center of revolutionary activities by Cuban immigrants who sought independence from Spain. José Martí, a writer and political activist who is Cuba's national hero, often traveled to Tampa from New York to raise money from cigar makers who supported Cuba's quest for independence.

José Martí fought for Cuba's independence from Spain for many years.

In 1895, revolutionaries had raised enough money to begin Cuba's second major war for independence. Martí landed on the eastern coast of Cuba that April with a small force to fight the Spanish army. He was killed soon afterward, and the war dragged on for three more years until the United States got involved. This started the Spanish-

American War of 1898. In a few short weeks, Spain was defeated and the United States took control of Cuba.

In Tampa, tensions had built up between Cubans and Spaniards right from the founding of Ybor City. It was to be expected, since Cubans were fighting to free themselves of Spain's rule. Sometimes the rivalry turned violent. "Ybor City is bitterly divided into two groups: Cubans and Spaniards," wrote Consuelo Stebbins in *City of Intrigue, Nest of Revolution.* She told of one riot in 1887 "that left one dead and four wounded."

Cubans fight during a revolution that began in 1895. Yet in some ways it was a family fight. Many of the Cuban activists, including Martí himself, were the sons or

daughters of Spaniards. "The Cubans, while they were bitter in their resentment of Spanish colonial repression, were heavily endowed with Spanish heritage," notes Frank Trebín Lastra in *Ybor City: The Making of a Landmark Town*. "They were enemies and brothers at the same time."

After the war ended, the United States ruled Cuba until 1902, when Cuba elected a president and became an independent nation. There was no more need to plot the war for independence, so the Cuban revolutionary clubs in the United States closed. Many Cubans returned to their newly independent country. But political instability in Cuba grew in 1906, when the United States sent in troops to put down a revolt and to take over the government temporarily. Many recently returned Cubans moved back to Tampa. Newly arrived Spaniards, who had lived in Cuba until its independence, also added to Tampa's population. Many of them had lived in Cuba and, after it became independent, decided to make a new life in Tampa.

For a while, many Spaniards in Tampa resented Cubans and Americans for stripping Spain of its colonies. On the other hand, Tampa's Cubans had unpleasant memories of being ruled by Spain with little say in the governing of their own country. So there was tension in town as the 1900s began.

Eventually *Tampeños*, as the Spanish-speakers of Tampa called themselves, tried to forget past differences and to make economic progress.

The Boom Years

Making cigars was the most important economic activity in town. After all, it was Ybor City that made it possible for Tampa to grow beyond a handful of houses on a swamp. Tampa historian Trebín Lastra reported that just twenty years after the founding of Ybor, more than 220 million cigars were manufactured. In 1929, the industry hit its peak, with nearly 505 million cigars made that year in Tampa.

In the golden period between 1900, just after the end of the Spanish-American War, and 1929, when the Great Depression started, those workers became an elite group. They were paid well enough to devote leisure time to cultural activities. Theaters enriched the lives of Tampeños, factory workers and factory managers alike. Spanish and Cuban diplomats also attended the shows. Performers of popular

A Cuban dance club photo from 1912 shows that immigrants had enough time and money at that time to devote some of it to cultural activities.

Cuban music gave concerts in Tampa, and famous operas such as *Rigoletto* and *La Traviata* were staged.

The center of Ybor City's cultural life, however, was the Cuban and Spanish American social clubs. These were major civic institutions with large buildings and memberships. They held banquets and dances in elegant ballrooms, where families got together and unmarried people met in a socially acceptable setting. The clubs also offered classes in Spanish and the history of Cuba or Spain, and some offered lifelong health care for members.

One of the most important clubs was the Centro Español, which was founded in 1891 but hit its period of big growth after the end of the Spanish-American War. Trebín Lastra quotes from an eyewitness account, "On December 31, 1900 . . . the Centro Español gave a grand ball at which the guests of honor were the local public officials and the most socially prominent Cubans." In 1904, a hospital was built for members, and in 1912, a new clubhouse and theater were built in the heart of Ybor City. By the following year, membership had grown so much that a second facility was built in nearby West Tampa.

Cubans founded similar social organizations. Now that Cuba's independence had been achieved, Cuban Tampeños turned to culture and entertainment. The major Cuban social club was the Círculo Cubano, founded in the 1890s. Its building featured a 1,500-seat theater, a library, and a classroom. It was built in 1905 after a groundbreaking ceremony attended by the mayor of Tampa and the *consuls* of Cuba, Spain, and Italy. The structure burned down in 1916, but a new and even larger building replaced it two years later.

The Círculo Cubano helped make Cubans feel more at home in Tampa. Those good feelings extended to the neighborhoods where people lived and shopped. "My mother went to work at 2:30 in the morning," recalled one man who grew up in Ybor City in the early 1900s, as quoted in *The Immigrant World of Ybor City*, by Gary R. Mormino and George

An advertisement from 1917 for the Cuban social club, Círculo Cubano.

E. Pozzetta. "She had to leave in the dark, at times carrying two of us with bottles of milk. No one ever bothered her, nor did we ever hear of someone being bothered." Along La Séptima, the main commercial street, shoppers made their way from chain stores such as Woolworth's to locally owned hardware stores and cleaners. They ate at bakeries and restaurants that served traditional Cuban and Spanish dishes.

Within Ybor City, Spanish-speaking immigrants found almost all they needed to preserve their culture, from music to food to people who spoke the same language and shared a similar culture.

ETHNIC TENSIONS

Yet all was not ideal. There were tensions between the ethnic groups inside Ybor City and the ethnic groups outside of it.

Cubans of African descent, for instance, had their own social clubs. The first and largest was the Unión Martí-Maceo, named for José Martí and Antonio Maceo. Maceo was a black Cuban general killed in the war of independence against Spain. Black Cubans worked in the tobacco factories along with the other Spanish-speakers. They also lived in the same neighborhoods as white Cubans and Spaniards. This scandalized native white American southerners, who had grown up with a system of racial segregation that Cubans did not follow.

There were also tensions among white Cubans, Spaniards, and Italians. Cubans and Spaniards never completely overcame their rivalries dating from the wars for independence. Spaniards, and Italians, too, viewed Cubans as undependable people who spent their money on having a good time rather than saving for the future. Cubans thought Spaniards were unfriendly and looked at Italians as unrefined because they had come from rural parts of Italy. There was *residential segregation*, too. Italians lived in the eastern half of Ybor City, while Spaniards and Cubans lived in the western half.

Yet there was overlap, and as the three groups continued to live together, they started to develop a common "Latin" identity. That happened partly because of the way they were treated by Anglos—the non-Hispanic, non-Italian whites who lived outside Ybor City. Many of these southern Americans saw Cuban, Spanish, and Italian workers as too emotional, impulsive, and un-American—the Latin stereotype. One newspaper complained that Cubans had "very little decency." Another made fun of Italians: "We don't want no Mafia in Tampa!" said one headline.

This caused the three "Latin" groups to band together. One Italian, resident in the early 1900s, quoted by Mormino and Pozzetta, recalled going to dances only to find signs banning him from going in. "No Italians, no Spanish, no Cubans, nothing!" he said. "But the Italian boys and the Spanish boys and the Cuban boys used to go in there and fight." Added one Hispanic man who also grew up in Tampa, "We were at the bottom of persons allowed— and we built Tampa!"

LABOR STRIKES

Another source of unrest was the conflict between owners of cigar factories and the *labor unions* that represented workers. There were twenty-three strikes in Tampa between 1887 and 1894 even though there was no central union to represent all workers.

That had changed by the early 1900s. Cigar workers had come together under the Cigar Makers' International Union (CMIU), a member of a nationwide group of unions called the American Federation of Labor. Meanwhile, the factory owners banded together in an organization called the Tampa Cigar Manufacturers Association.

What made labor-management relations especially tense was that radical groups from Spain, Cuba, Italy, and northern American cities had come to Ybor City to recruit workers. These groups included *communists*, who believed private property should be illegal, and *anarchists*, who wanted to get rid of government completely.

The cigar factory owners were *capitalists*. They were strong believers in a government that protected private property—so they were opposed to both communism and

Employees hand roll cigars in a cigar factory in Ybor City in Florida.

anarchism. The radicals also clashed with the views of most workers, who simply wanted a union that helped them make a good living.

Both radicals and workers were unhappy when factory owners cut wages in 1910. By that time, some local owners had sold their factories to national companies such as American Tobacco, which employed 20 percent of tobacco workers. In August 1910, more than twelve thousand workers either walked off their jobs to protest lower pay or were shut out of work by factory owners trying to force them to accept the lower wages.

As the strike went on, there was violence between workers and members of the Citizens Committee. This committee consisted mostly of white businessmen and professionals who believed the strike would hurt Tampa's cigar-dependent economy. Seven months after the strike started, many workers faced the violent tactics of the Citizens Committee as well as the economic pressure of being out of work. The strikers voted to return to work and accept the lower pay.

Another strike took place in 1920, when CMIU told its members to walk off the job unless owners would require that every new employee join the union. A few factory owners responded by buying cigar-making machines to replace workers. It was a hint of things to come.

In 1929, the Great Depression began, and Tampa's cigar industry suffered. Thousands of cigar makers were laid off

Mass Meeting Celebrando el
Sexto Mes de Huelga
Tampa Fla 14 de Oct 1920

as factories replaced workers with machines or simply
closed down. The unemployed workers had little money to
spend, so local retail stores also suffered. Shops on La
Séptima, which had thrived during the 1920s, faced a large
loss in business. Trebín Lastra, who was a child in Ybor City
during the Depression, wrote that "There was no money
for new socks, dresses, pants or shoes. Holes in socks were

A mass meeting
of cigar workers
during the strike
of 1920.

Members of an anarchist militia wave their flags and rifles during the Spanish Civil War.

solved easily: simply pull the socks down a notch. Pants or dresses too short? Mom had a sewing machine."

Meanwhile, in Spain, a civil war began in 1936. On one side were the Loyalists, made up of republicans, socialists, communists, and anarchists who were part of an elected government; on the other were the Nationalists, made up of monarchists, conservative Catholics, and fascists who tried to overthrow them. The Spaniards of Ybor City mostly supported the elected government. They donated "at least two ambulances, millions of cigarettes, tons of beans, clothing, medical supplies and much needed cash," Trebín Lastran wrote. The Nationalists won the war, which ended in 1939.

By that time, the economic situation had improved in Tampa as well as in the entire country. Yet Tampa never recovered its old standing as a center for the manufacture of cigars. Cigar smoking became less popular, more machines replaced workers, and factories closed. Ybor City became a forgotten neighborhood until recent times, when it was reborn as a tourist attraction. Today visitors come to see what the old days in Tampa were like, when Cubans and Spaniards sometimes fought each other and sometimes helped each other, but always worked together to make cigars.

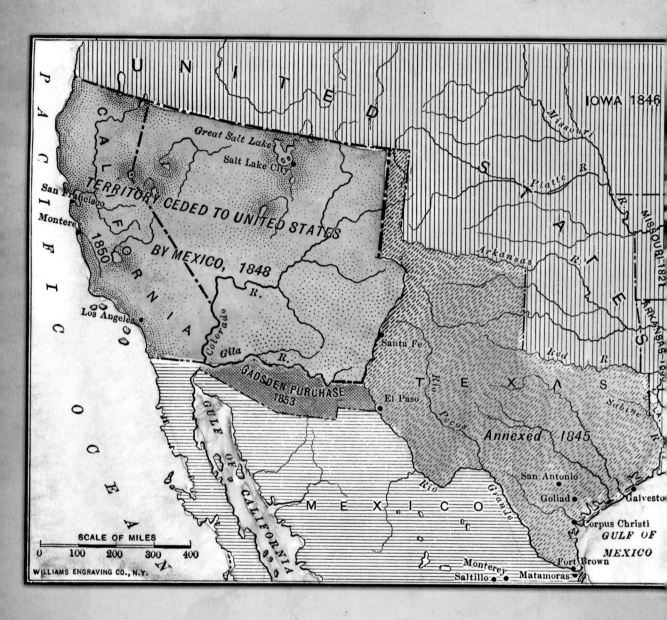

CHAPTER THREE

MEXICAN IMMIGRATION BEGINS

I N 1846, THE MEXICAN-AMERICAN WAR BROKE out between the United States and Mexico after the United States *annexed* Texas, which once had been Mexican territory. Mexico was defeated, and the United States acquired much of what would become the states of Arizona, California, Colorado, Nevada, New Mexico, Texas, Utah, and Wyoming. With that territory came the Spanish-speaking people who lived in it—tens of thousands of former Mexican citizens who suddenly became citizens of the United States.

Nobody really knows how many such Hispanics lived in the United States by the early 1900s, two generations after the war. The U.S. Census Bureau did not keep track of Hispanic ethnicity then. But it did count foreign-born residents, and in 1900 the bureau counted just over 100,000 Mexican-born

Opposite: This map shows the territory Mexico lost to the United States during the Mexican-American War.

These Mexican Americans lived in Texas and here, they prepare a meal outside their small shack.

people living in the United States. The great majority lived in the Southwest—almost 6,600 in New Mexico, about 8,000 in California, about 14,000 in Arizona, and more than 70,000 in Texas.

There were even more Hispanics, counting those born in the United States. A sizable number came from families that had lived in New Mexico ever since the area was settled by Spain in the 1600s. Others were *Tejanos* and *Californios*—Spanish-speakers whose families had lived in

Texas and California before the regions became part of the United States. Still, the growth of the Southwest's Hispanic population in those first few decades of the 1900s was a result of new Mexican immigration to the United States.

Before 1910, few Mexicans immigrated. In the big industrial cities of the North, immigrants from Europe—more than 10 million arrived between 1900 and 1910—caused controversy. Some people said the United States was letting in too many foreigners. But in the Southwest, in the early twentieth century, few people seemed to mind Mexicans crossing the border.

A report from U.S. Citizenship and Immigration Services, the government agency that regulates immigration, says that in 1900 there were only four U.S. inspectors working along the Mexican border, at Nogales, Arizona; El Paso and Laredo, Texas; and Piedras Negras, Mexico. Their records showed an annual average of fewer than five hundred Mexicans entering the United States between 1900 and 1905. This number is so impossibly low that it means almost nobody bothered to count, probably because so many Mexicans passed back and forth between the two countries to see family or to work. Even as late as 1908, when a more thorough system of inspection was set up, the main targets were immigrants smuggled through Mexico from countries such as Syria, Greece, Japan, and China. As for Mexicans themselves, "The majority . . . were questioned at the port, recorded, and admitted."

THE FIRST BIG WAVE

The year 1910 marked a watershed in the history of Mexico, as well as in the history of Mexican immigration to the United States. In the presidential election that year Porfirio Díaz, who had governed harshly since 1876, committed fraud to stay in power. His opponent, Francisco Madero, backed by leaders Emiliano Zapata and Pancho Villa, launched a revolt and unseated Díaz. Madero became president, but he was assassinated in 1913. Mexico plunged into more than a decade of violent political turmoil. Scholars have estimated that more than a million Mexicans lost their lives because of the conflict.

Life in Mexico became so unbearable for many that for the first time Mexicans migrated to the United States in massive numbers. An estimated 890,000 Mexicans entered the United States between 1910 and 1920. As in the past, many did not set out to be permanent U.S. residents but simply crossed the border back and forth. Yet the settled Mexican American population grew. In 1920, the year of the first full U.S. census after the Mexican Revolution, 486,000 people of Mexican birth were counted in the

Porfirio Díaz was reelected president of Mexico in 1910, but under suspicious conditions. He was soon unseated and replaced by Francisco Madero.

BECOMING U.S. CITIZENS

Like most immigrant groups, the first Mexicans who came to the United States worked in backbreaking jobs that paid little. Historian George Sánchez reported that about 90 percent of Mexican immigrants between 1900 and 1930 held blue-collar jobs. According to one study, 70 percent were unskilled laborers.

Sánchez conducted his own study of immigrants who applied to become U.S. citizens around the same period. He determined that they fared better economically than immigrants who had not applied for citizenship. A quarter of them had white-collar jobs, and of the blue-collar workers fewer than than 30 percent were *unskilled laborers*.

United States—more than five times the population at the beginning of the century.

Mexicans settled in cities on or near the border. By 1920, about 30,500 of El Paso's 77,000 residents were Mexican born—the largest Mexican population of any American city. San Antonio was next, at nearly 28,500 out of 80,700. There were probably many more people of Mexican ancestry in those towns, because the census bureau did not count U.S.-born Mexican Americans.

Mexicans had an easier time entering the United States than other immigrants. For one thing, they only had to cross a land border, marked in most of its length by the shallow Rio Grande. In contrast, Europeans and Asians had to cross an ocean. Even immigrants from Cuba and Puerto Rico could only arrive on American soil after sailing in ships. Mexicans could simply walk in.

Mexicans also had fewer legal barriers. The Immigration Acts of 1921 and 1924 severely decreased the number of immigrants allowed to enter the United States, especially from eastern and southern Europe. Asian immigration had been drastically cut back by that time, too, with the Chinese Exclusion Act of 1882 and the "Gentlemen's Agreement" of 1907, which basically eliminated immigration from Japan. But there were no laws aimed at slowing Mexican immigration.

One reason was the demand for workers. Historian George Sánchez wrote in his book *Becoming Mexican American* that before the Great Depression, California and the Southwest had booms in jobs digging mines, building railroads, and working on farms. These jobs paid as much as two dollars a day—"far above the 12 cents a day paid on several of the rural *haciendas* of central Mexico," but less than many Americans earned. So the employers made bigger profits because they could pay Mexican workers less.

Employers were so eager to find more Mexican workers that they set up networks of employment agencies in border towns. These labor recruiters also went into Mexico to sign people to work contracts. This was illegal—foreign workers could only be hired after they migrated. But the federal government, in charge of regulating immigration, chose to ignore these practices, because officials wanted to help American employers looking for workers.

Many Mexicans were eager to take up the offer. Mexicans who fled to the United States earned much more money and got to escape the violence of the revolution. For some brief moments, though, that violence crossed the border into the United States.

REVOLUTIONARIES IN THE UNITED STATES

In January 1915, authorities in Texas uncovered a plot that some Mexican Americans had to form a Liberating Army of Races and Peoples. The plot's leaders sought to recruit Mexican Americans, African Americans, and Japanese Americans. The purpose of the Plan de San Diego, as it was called, was to take over the states of Arizona, California,

Colorado, New Mexico and Texas, to form an independent country, and eventually to seek annexation to Mexico.

Although some of the leaders were arrested, others managed to lead raids in South Texas. They killed whites, destroyed railroad tracks, and cut telephone and telegraph lines. Many white Texans believed Mexican Americans were traitors who wanted to reconquer the territory that the United States had taken in the Mexican-American War of 1846.

That August, raiders led by conspirator Luis de la Rosa attacked King Ranch, which was famous for being a leader in ranching practices and education, as well as for its size of 825,000 acres (333,866 hectares). Texas historian Robert Mendoza wrote, "This time, de la Rosa had gone too far, attacking the grandest and most *venerable* symbol of Anglo

The Texas Rangers, a statewide police agency, looked to stop the Mexicans who wanted to liberate Texas and other states from the U.S.'s control.

dominance in South Texas." The top officers in the Texas Rangers, the statewide police agency, began to hunt for de la Rosa and his men. He "managed to slip away from the posse but many innocent Mexicanos in the vicinity of Norias were shot down," wrote Mendoza. Tensions rose as rangers received official instructions to "shoot to disable any suspicious character on sight."

Law enforcement officials certainly had to respond to outlaws who murdered people. But many historians today believe the Texas Rangers overreacted. The rangers' own official museum states that during this period "the Ranger force grew to its largest level, but the lack of training and controls were evident. Some of the new companies upheld the law while others functioned as *vigilante* groups [angered] by raids from Mexico." Even at the time, officials recognized something had gone wrong: "After one . . . Ranger raid into Mexico, an entire company was dismissed. In one battle in 1917, as many as 20 Mexicans may have been killed by Rangers who crossed into Mexico," the Texas Ranger museum website says.

What little support there was for the Plan de San Diego disappeared. It did not have the support of a large part of the Mexican American community.

The Plan de San Diego remained local. But a different raid turned into an international issue. In 1916 Mexican revolutionary Pancho Villa attacked the town of Columbus, New Mexico, with about five hundred armed civilians. They

Pancho Villa
was a Mexican
revolutionary
who formed an
army of civilians
and attacked
the town of
Columbus,
New Mexico.

killed U.S. Army soldiers stationed there and burned down much of the center of town.

Historians are not sure why Villa attacked Columbus. One theory says it was because U.S. president Woodrow Wilson supported Villa's enemy, President Venustiano Carranza. Another theory is that Villa intended to force two Columbus arms dealers to provide Villa's troops with guns and ammunition that Villa had paid for but not received. A third theory is that Villa also needed food, clothing, and other supplies.

Whatever his motivation, Villa was a major political figure in Mexico's ongoing revolution, unlike the petty criminals of the Plan de San Diego. So on orders from President Wilson, ten thousand U.S. troops marched into Mexico to capture Villa. They drove in as far as 300 miles (480 km) and fought little battles along the way. The Americans fought not only Villa's supporters but also forces led by Villa's enemy and Wilson's one-time ally, Carranza. Neither Villa nor Carranza wanted U.S. troops on Mexican territory. The American expedition never did find Villa, and it returned to the United States after a campaign of eleven months.

GOING TO CALIFORNIA

The turmoil of the Mexican Revolution began to die down in the early 1920s, but immigration did not stop. There was less violence to flee in Mexico, but there was just as much poverty. Salaries in the United States were higher, and employers continued to look for Mexican laborers. Immigration from Europe and Asia had been cut drastically, so during the 1920s, Mexican immigrants made up nearly 16 percent of all immigrants—the highest proportion up to that time. The 1930 census—the first that counted both Mexicans born in Mexico and U.S.-born Mexican Americans—reported that there were 1.42 million people of Mexican descent in the United States.

The major point of entry in the early years of the century had been Texas. The state had good railway connections, and there was already a substantial Mexican population as early as 1910. The population there continued to grow—to nearly 684,000 by 1930, the census said. By then large numbers of Mexican immigrants were also moving to California. Salaries were higher there. In *Becoming Mexican American*, historian George Sánchez wrote that in the late 1920s Mexican cotton pickers were earning $1.75 a day in Texas and $3.25 in California.

The most popular California destination was Los Angeles, where employers developed agencies to recruit Mexican workers. Overall, Los Angeles had grown spectacularly. In 1890, it was a middle-size town of 50,000 inhabitants. In 1930, it was the nation's fifth-largest city, with 1.2 million residents—and a total of 2.2 million in the entire *metropolitan area*. The Mexican population also grew, from 20,000 in 1920 to 97,000 in 1930.

Many Mexicans immigrated to California, and Los Angeles was a popular destination. Here, a cobbler sets up shop near the Los Angeles City Hall.

Californios, the Spanish-speakers who lived in the region before the United States took control of it, had practically disappeared as a distinct community by the 1920s. They had either left the area or had intermarried with the Anglo community, so there was little contact between new Mexican immigrants and old-time Californios.

But the newcomers did inherit an old Hispanic tradition. One of the neighborhoods in which Mexican immigrants settled was the *Plaza de la Reyna de Los Angeles* (the Town of the Queen of the Angels). This city square marks the founding of the present-day city of Los Angeles in 1781, when California and the Southwest were part of the

Spanish empire. The square was filled with stores that sold Mexican food and other goods.

Mexican immigrants lived in other neighborhoods toward the east of the city. Mexicans, blacks, Asians, and Jews lived together on that side of town, while Anglos lived toward the west. Few people on the east side were wealthy, but at least many had jobs during the economically booming 1920s.

That came crashing to a halt, however, with the Great Depression in 1929.

GOING BACK HOME

The Great Depression that began in 1929 was a period of very high unemployment and economic ruin throughout the world. It lasted about ten years. It came after the decade of the 1920s, a time of general economic health.

The economic well-being of the 1920s was one reason why Mexican immigrants were in demand in the United States. Employers had plenty of jobs, and they sought to pay low salaries. Once those jobs disappeared, though, many people turned on immigrants. Some native-born Americans felt immigrants were taking too many of the available jobs. Immigrants from Mexico, in particular, were targeted. Federal and state governments, aided by many citizens groups, began a policy of *repatriation*. Through this policy, some Mexican immigrants and even Mexican Americans were encouraged to leave the United States

During the Great Depression, many people suffered with little or no money, including immigrants. Here, a migrant Mexican field-worker stands outside his home in California.

and move to Mexico. Others were simply forced out.

Francisco Balderrama and Raymond Rodríguez, in their book *Decade of Betrayal*, estimate that up to one million people were forced out of the United States. About 60 percent were children born in the United States. The Texas State Historical Association estimates that about 400,000 to 500,000 Mexicans, along with their American-born children, went back to Mexico.

The repatriation campaign peaked in the early 1930s, the worst years of the Depression. Balderrama and Rodríguez reported that in one raid near Los Angeles, immigration agents "went door to door demanding that

When the repatriation policy was put into effect in the 1920s, Mexican immigrants were encouraged to leave the United States, even if they had children who were born in the United States and were therefore U.S. citizens.

Mexican residents produce [proof] of legal residency. Those unable to do so were arrested and taken to jail."

Others decided on their own that the time had come to leave the United States. Farmworkers suffered in the economic chaos. Cotton pickers, who earned an average of

$1.21 per 100 pounds (45 kg) of cotton picked in 1928, saw their wages dip to 44 cents in 1931. "Mexican laborers simply could not live on such low wages," says a report from the Texas State Historical Association. City dwellers suffered, too. "Owners of small commercial enterprises, artisans, and professional persons were severely harmed by the depression," the same report says. "Their financial problems were compounded by the repatriation or deportation of thousands of customers."

Another problem was that the U.S.-born people who were forced to leave only knew life in the United States. They felt like foreigners in Mexico. Children in Mexico teased American-born children. "They were not allowed to forget that they had been rejected—kicked out—by the land of their birth, and were actually kids without a homeland," wrote Balderrama and Rodríguez. Children who could not speak Spanish well were bullied.

As the 1930s wore on, the Great Depression eased and the economy slowly returned to normal. The repatriation programs ended, and some Mexicans—nobody really knows how many—returned to the United States. In the following decade, many Mexican Americans gained respect fighting as Americans in World War II. And with the economy booming, the U.S. government reversed its policy of repatriating immigrants. In 1942, U.S. and Mexican officials signed an agreement that eventually brought four million Mexican laborers to work the farms of America.

CHAPTER FOUR

OLD CULTURE IN NEW MEXICO

N EW MEXICO IS A UNIQUE PLACE FOR THE Spanish-speaking people of the United States. Only New Mexico has a Hispanic community whose culture has survived without interruption for four hundred years—since before the United States even existed. The presence of that culture dates from the time the first Spanish colonists settled northern New Mexico in 1598. The seat of government, Santa Fe, officially became a capital of the territory in 1610. This makes it the oldest capital city in the United States.

The entire Southwest was part of Spain's overseas empire until the 1820s, when Mexico won its independence from Spain. Then the Southwest became part of Mexico. After the United States defeated Mexico in the war of 1846 to 1848, Americans claimed the territory. Language historian James

Opposite: A New Mexican family stands in the field they farm.

Crawford wrote that some 75,000 Spanish-speaking people lived in the Southwest at the time—1,000 in Arizona, 1,500 in Colorado, 5,000 in Texas, 7,500 in California, and 60,000 in New Mexico. The communities of Californios and Tejanos disappeared little by little in the second half of the nineteenth century, as families intermarried with Anglos or simply moved away. The few thousand descendants of early Spanish settlers in Arizona and Colorado had a similar fate. Today most of the Hispanic people who live in the Southwest are new immigrants or the descendants of immigrants who started arriving after the Mexican Revolution of 1910.

But in New Mexico the story was very different. The colonial-era population was much larger, and its descendants still form a distinct community today. They have lived for generations in old Spanish cities such as Santa Fe or in the small villages near the Sangre de Cristo Mountains.

A DISTINCT CULTURE

During the first fifty or sixty years after New Mexico became part of the United States, some of its Spanish-speaking people—especially those who lived in the more isolated areas—had little contact with other Americans. For many years they kept their traditions and used the Spanish language. An 1876 report on education in New Mexico said that Spanish and English were taught in 12 schools in the territory, while in 111 schools instruction was in Spanish

New Mexican children were spoken to in Spanish in school even after New Mexico became part of the United States.

OLD CULTURE IN NEW MEXICO

63

only. As late as 1928, almost all the instruction was in Spanish. The use of Spanish was just the most obvious signs that *Nuevomexicanos* (New Mexicans) held on to their ancestral culture. Life in New Mexico differed from life in most of the United States in other ways, too. For instance, the extended family was "the most important single factor in the social organization" of small towns wrote author Nancie L. González in *The Spanish-Americans of New Mexico*. "Most Hispanos would include other relatives besides parents and siblings as members of their *familias*; grandparents, parents' siblings and [their] children, termed *primo hermanos*, are all considered 'close relatives.'" One study of a rural village completed in 1936 said that "all emigrating family members are kept track of forever . . . even if they spend all of their time in larger towns such as Albuquerque or Phoenix."

Another tradition was the Penitentes, a Catholic religious society rooted in medieval Spain. In New Mexico, these groups came into existence in the nineteenth century to perform in public Catholic ceremonies when there was a shortage of priests. The Penitentes—who still exist today—led groups in prayer, offered spiritual advice, and organized religious festivities. They are most famous for the reenactment of processions during Holy Week, including a reenactment of Christ's crucifixion on Good Friday.

There were economic differences, too. New Mexico's

THE SPANISH LANGUAGE

Although New Mexico received few immigrants from Mexico, the old families from Spanish colonial days managed to hold on to the Spanish language, at least through the 1930s. Most school instruction was in Spanish, and in 1931 there were at least nine weekly newspapers and an illustrated monthly published in Spanish, according to sociologist Nancie L. González.

Then New Mexico's own Hispanic leaders made a push to teach more people English. "I love Spanish traditions, I love the people and ancestors I hail from," said Senator Dennis Chávez in 1932, "[but] I insist that in New Mexico the teaching of English should be stressed." The next generation learned English. Children sometimes had trouble communicating with grandparents who only spoke Spanish. It was a major cultural shift.

economy was still based on sheep and cattle raising, while much of the rest of the country became industrialized in the late nineteenth century. As late as 1908, for instance, the population of Albuquerque, New Mexico's largest city, was only ten thousand people. Even when factory jobs began to open in New Mexico in the early 1900s, some traditional ranchers continued to raise livestock.

The survival of Hispano culture is even more remarkable given the fact that it thrived without much help from

In the 1900s, cattle ranching was still popular in New Mexico.

freshly arrived immigrants from Mexico. From 1880 to 1920, only 7 percent of New Mexico's population was foreign born. After that the proportion actually declined, to only 3 percent in 1940. The culture, language and traditions lived on through families who had stayed on their land for generations.

STATEHOOD BATTLE

Although Nuevomexicanos were culturally distinct from other Americans, and even though some Hispano families remained isolated, upper-class Hispano families had friendly relations with many whites. Intermarriages were common, as were business partnerships and political alliances. Author Richard Nostrand, in his book *The Hispano Homeland*, wrote that in the heart of New Mexico at the turn of the century, "Hispanos and Anglos shared in political control, social prestige and the rewards of economic activity."

But there were sources of tension. Some Anglos felt that Nuevomexicanos, as Spanish-speaking Catholics, were just too different from the mainstream to ever be "real Americans." So, for more than sixty years, they worked to keep New Mexico a territory instead of a full state.

Not all Anglos had this prejudice. During the 1870s and 1880s, the Santa Fe Ring, a group of Anglo and Nuevomexicano lawyers, politicians, and landowners, led a statehood effort that was approved by New Mexico's legislature. But two years later, Congress voted down the statehood proposal. Politicians in New Mexico did not give up—and they had powerful allies. One of them was President William McKinley, who traveled to New Mexico in 1901 to show support for Governor Miguel Otero—New Mexico's first Hispanic governor and a strong supporter of statehood.

"My friend says you want to be connected with us," said McKinley about Otero and statehood. "You are of us and close to us. The flag flies over you as it floats over all . . . I do not know when, but some time in the future the Congress of the United States will see fit to make you a state."

But opposition built up. "Why has New Mexico thus far knocked upon the doors of the Union in vain?" asks a *New York Times* article from 1905. The article suggests that part of the reason was that "in the towns it is useless to ask one's way in English . . . an American visitor meets conditions under the American flag that make him feel he is in a foreign land."

Perhaps to water down the idea of admitting a "Spanish state," in 1906 Congress passed a bill that offered joint statehood to Arizona and New Mexico. At the time, about half of New Mexico residents were Spanish speaking, but in Arizona the estimate was 5 to 20 percent. But the statehood bill could only become effective if passed by voters in both territories. In Arizona, the legislature passed a resolution saying that joint statehood "would subject us to the domination of another commonwealth of different traditions, customs and aspirations." When the vote came, joint

Miguel Otero was New Mexico's first Hispanic governor.

statehood won in New Mexico but lost in Arizona, so neither became a state.

Yet prostatehood New Mexicans, Anglo and Hispanic alike, did not give up the fight—and they had another ally in President William H. Taft. He pressured Congress to pass a law that authorized a New Mexico constitutional convention

to prepare for statehood. The delegates drafted a new state constitution, which voters approved in 1911. Then, on January 6, 1912, Taft signed the proclamation admitting New Mexico as the forty-seventh state. Sixty-two years had passed since it had became a U.S. territory.

HOLDING ON

Even after it became the forty-seventh state, New Mexico retained Spanish as a co-official language with English. Nuevomexicanos tried to hold on to their culture, even as New Mexico itself was changing. In 1900, there were 120,000 Spanish-speakers in New Mexico, and they outnumbered Anglos three to one. Within ten years, the non-Hispanic white population had grown to 282,000, due to the large number of people who had moved to New Mexico from other parts of the United States. Whites and Nuevomexicanos sometimes competed, and sometimes cooperated. For instance, in 1936, Dennis Chávez became the first Hispanic elected to the United States Senate, where he served until his death in 1962.

In the first half of the twentieth century, New Mexico's Hispanic community had found a way to be American while holding on to its roots. It held on to a statewide influence in culture, politics, and business that no Hispanic American community matched until recent times.

President William H. Taft signs New Mexico into statehood in 1912.

TIMELINE

1898	The Spanish-American War ends with the defeat of Spain and the U.S. takeover of Cuba and Puerto Rico.
1900	The Foraker Act establishes U.S. control over Puerto Rico, putting the island on the path to its current commonwealth status.
1902	Cuba becomes an independent nation.
1910	A revolution in Mexico plunges that country into a decade of political unrest, leading to a massive boom in Mexican migration to the U.S.
	Luis Muñoz Rivera, a leading Puerto Rican politician, is elected the island's resident commissioner to the U.S. House of Representatives.
	More than twelve thousand Tampa cigar factory workers go on strike to protest low pay.
1912	New Mexico and Arizona join the Union as the forty-seventh and forty-eighth states.
1915	A group of Mexican Americans plot the Plan de San Diego to take over several U.S. western states and territories. U.S. authorities stop the plan, but tensions between the U.S. and Mexico worsen.
1916	Mexican revolutionary Pancho Villa attacks the town of Columbus, New Mexico, killing U.S. soldiers stationed there and setting the town on fire.
1929	The U.S. stock market crashes, leading to the Great Depression, a tough economic period that lasts through the 1930s.
	Tampa's Ybor City cigar-manufacturing industry hits its peak, with nearly 505 million cigars produced in the city. The city's population grows to more than 100,000 the next year.
1930s	The U.S. government, responding to economic troubles, begins a policy of repatriation, encouraging or forcing hundreds of thousands of Mexican Americans to go back to Mexico.
1936	Dennis Chavez of New Mexico is the first Hispanic elected to the U.S. Senate; he served until 1962.
1937	Oscar Garcia Rivera is elected to the New York State Assembly, the first Puerto Rican elected to public office in the U.S.
1939	Germany invades Poland, starting World War II.

Glossary

anarchists People who are against government authority.

annexed (v) To incorporate a territory into the domain of a country.

armistice Temporary suspension of fighting between two sides.

assembly A legislative body that makes laws, usually at the state level.

capitalists People who support an economic system based on freedom to do business.

commonwealth In the case of Puerto Rico, a political arrangement midway between independence and full statehood.

communists People who follow a political system in which all property is owned by the government.

consuls Diplomatic representatives from one country to another.

discrimination When a person or group of people are mistreated because they are different.

fascism A political system that stresses the nation above individual rights.

Great Depression The devastating worldwide economic downturn from 1929 to about 1939.

hacienda A large estate.

labor unions Organizations that protect the rights of workers and seek fair wages.

metropolitan area A city and the suburbs near it.

monarchy A government led by a king or queen.

referenda Public votes on proposed laws.

repatriation To go back to one's country.

residential segregation The separation of neighborhoods on the basis of race or ethnicity.

sovereign Self-ruling, independent.

strike (v) To stop work in order to force an employer to agree to demands.

tenement housing Living quarters meeting the minimum standards of sanitation and comfort.

two-chamber legislature A lawmaking body with upper and lower groups, such as the U.S. House of Representatives and the Senate.

unskilled laborers Workers who lack technical training.

venerable Regarded with respect.

vigilante A volunteer who seeks to punish those who commit crimes.

FURTHER INFORMATION

BOOKS

Crompton, Samuel Willard. *The Sinking of the USS Maine* (Milestones in American History). New York: Chelsea House, 2008.

Hovius, Christopher. *Latino Migrant Workers: America's Harvesters* (Hispanic Heritage). Broomall, PA: Mason Crest, 2005.

King, David. *People at the Center of the Spanish-American War* (The Young People's History of American's Wars). Woodbridge, CT: Blackbirch Press, 2005.

WEBSITES

Welcome to Puerto Rico

http://welcome.topuertorico.org/index.shtml

Information on many Puerto Rican topics, including history, culture, government, and the economy

The Ybor City Museum Society

http://www.ybormuseum.org

A history of Ybor City

New Mexico Culturenet

http://www.nmculturenet.org

Artists, educators, writers, and technologists examine New Mexico's history and culture

BIBLIOGRAPHY

Balderrama, Francisco, and Raymond Rodríguez. *Decade of Betrayal*. Albuquerque: University of New Mexico Press, 2006.

Chenault, Lawrence R. *The Puerto Rican Migrant in New York City*. New York: Russell & Russell, 1938.

García, Alma. *The Mexicans*. Westport, CT: Greenwood Press, 2002.

González, Nancie L. *The Spanish-Americans of New Mexico*. Albuquerque: University of New Mexico Press, 2004.

Hernández, Roger E., and Alex Anton. *Cubans in America*. New York: Kensington Books, 2002.

Montgomery, Charles. *The Spanish Redemption*. Berkeley and Los Angeles: University of California Press, 2002.

Mormino, Gary R., and George E. Pozzetta. *The Immigrant World of Ybor City*. Urbana and Chicago: University of Illinois Press, 1987.

Nieto-Phillips, John M. *The Language of Blood*. Albuquerque: University of New Mexico Press, 2004.

Sánchez, George. *Becoming Mexican American*. New York: Oxford University Press, 1993.

Sánchez, José Ramón. *Boricua Power*. New York: New York University Press, 2007.

Stebbins, Consuelo E. *City of Intrigue, Nest of Revolution: A Documentary History of Key West in the Nineteenth Century*. Gainesville: University Press of Florida, 2007.

Trebín Lastra, Frank. *Ybor City: The Making of a Landmark Town*. Tampa: University of Tampa Press, 2006.

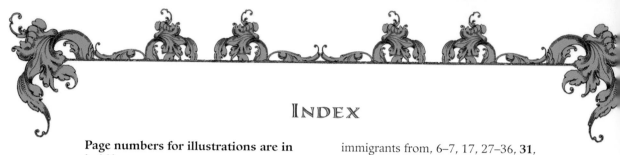

INDEX

ABOUT THE AUTHOR

ROGER E. HERNÁNDEZ writes a nationally syndicated column distributed by King Features to some forty daily newspapers across the country. He is also writer in residence at the New Jersey Institute of Technology and author of *Cubans in America*. Hernández was born in Cuba and came to the United States as a child in 1965, when his parents fled the Castro regime.